Inserting clipart images

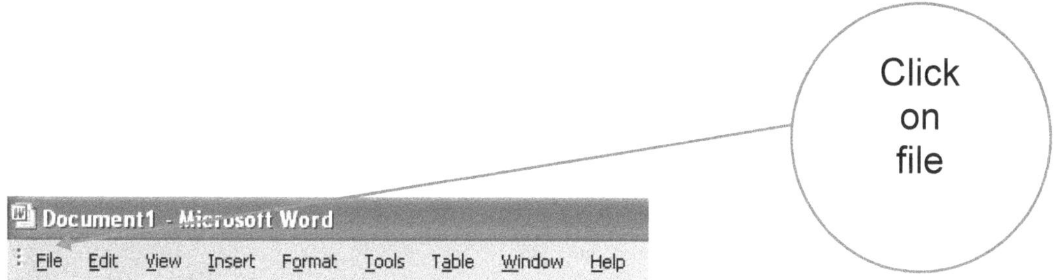

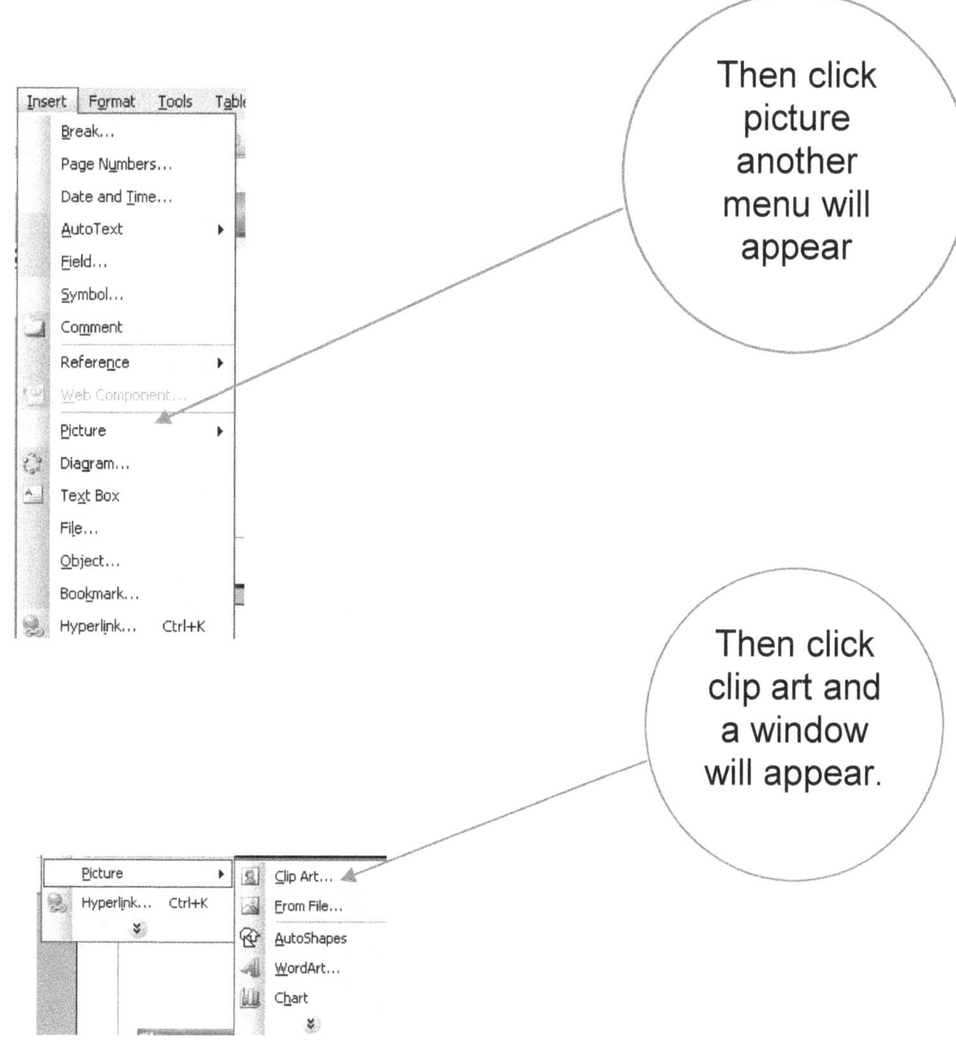

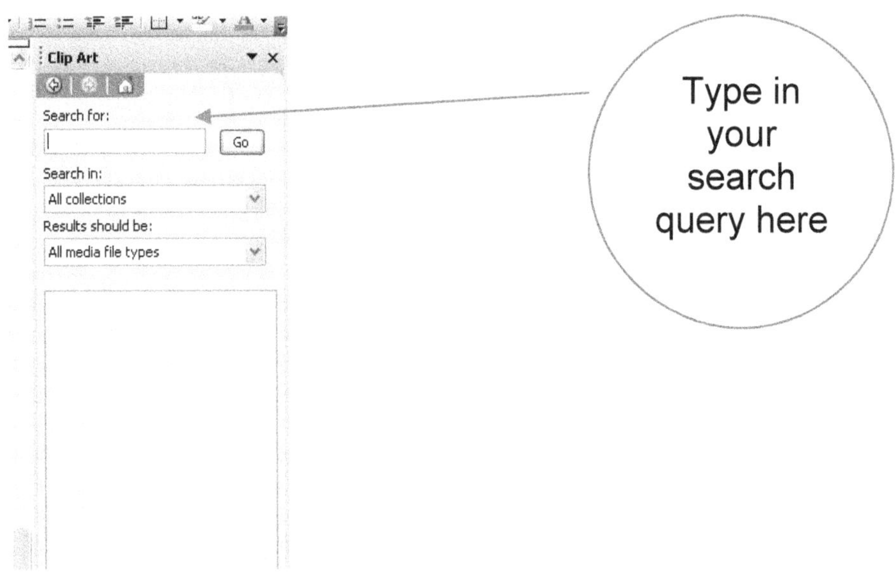
Clip Art
Search for:
Go
Search in:
All collections
Results should be:
All media file types
Type in your search query here

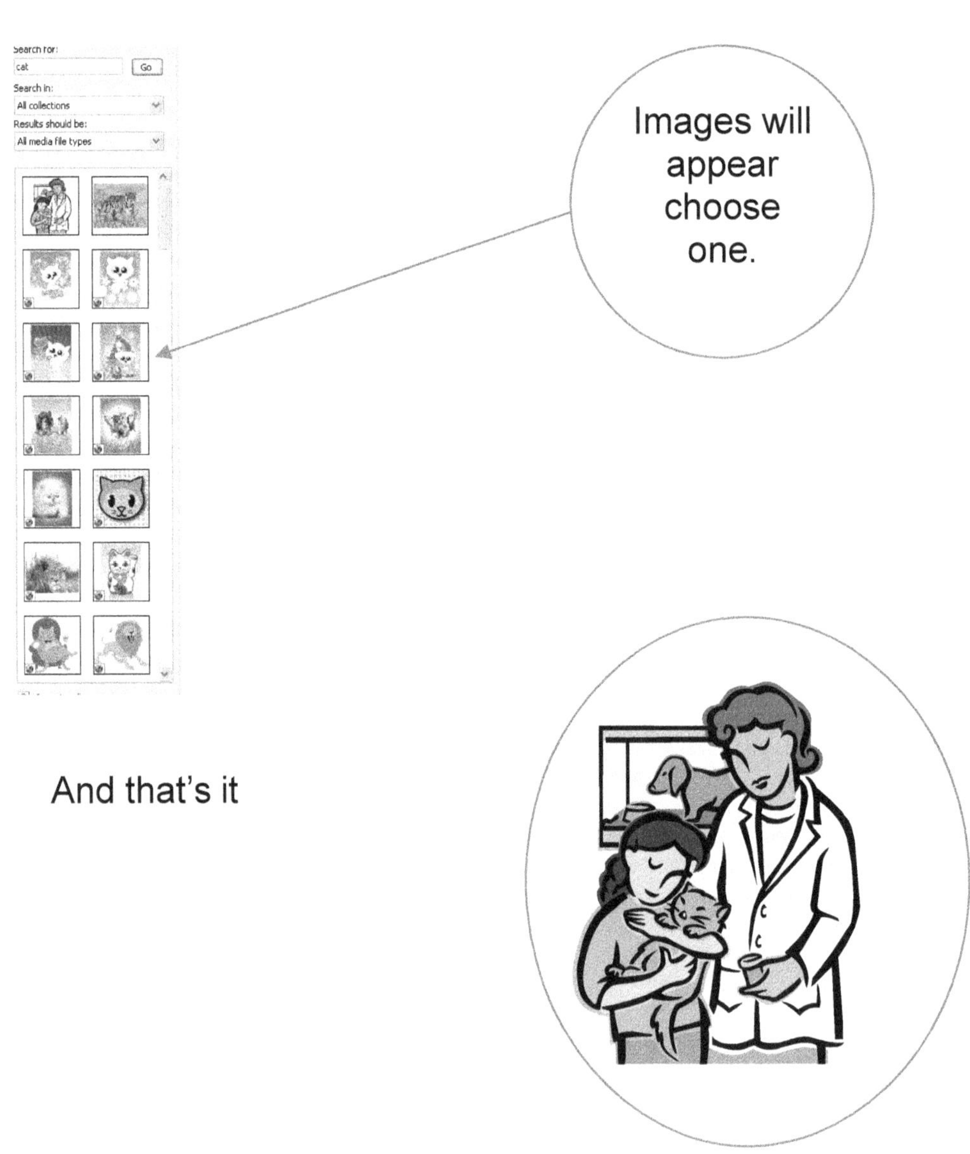
Search for:
cat
Go
Search in:
All collections
Results should be:
All media file types
Images will appear choose one.

And that's it

Inserting images from saved location

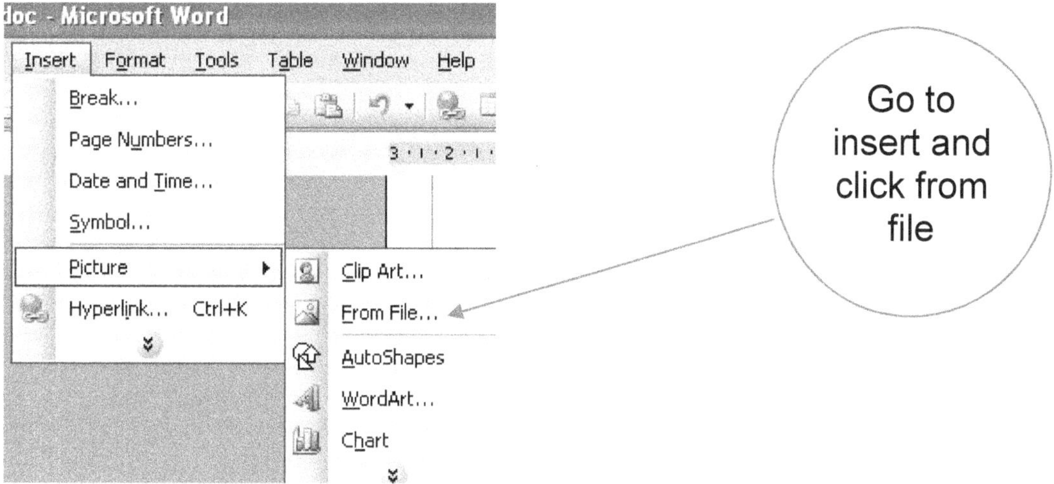

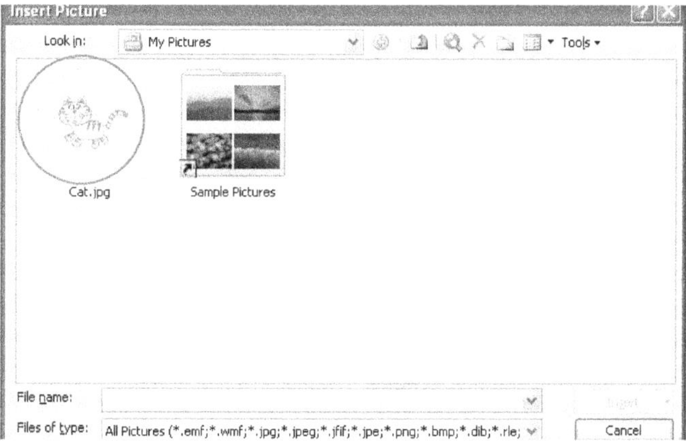

3rd double click on the file you want

And that's it

Importing from pen drive

Do up to step 2 but then click the arrow

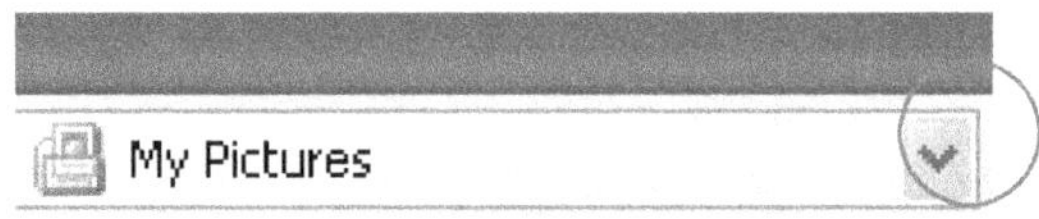

Then click the name of your memory stick in this case mines called jordan e 1n

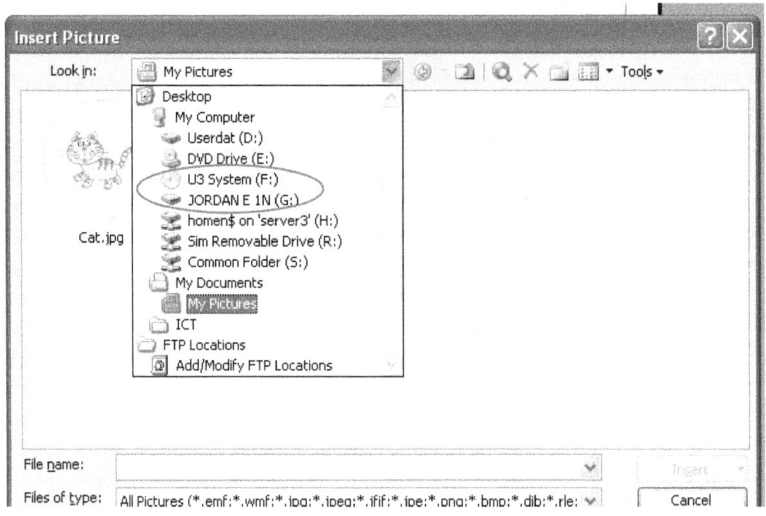

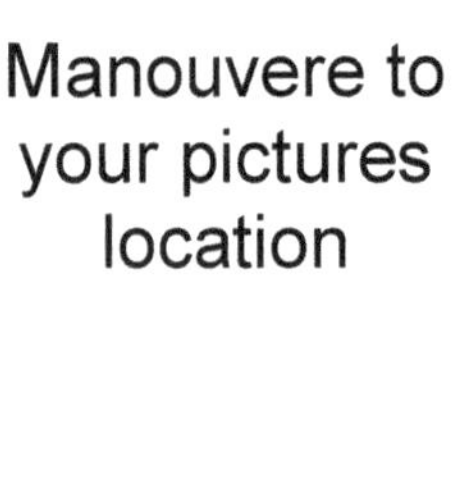

Manouvere to your pictures location

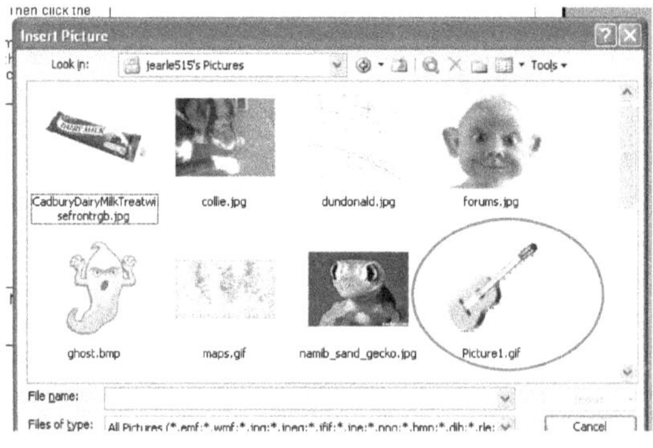

Double click on the flie you want

And that's it

Autoshapes

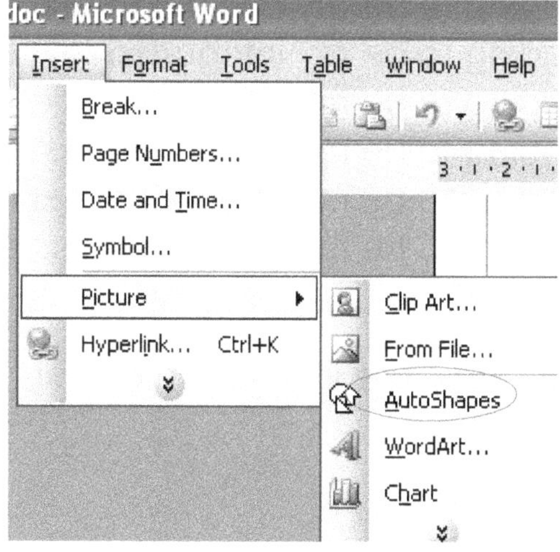

Click autoshapes

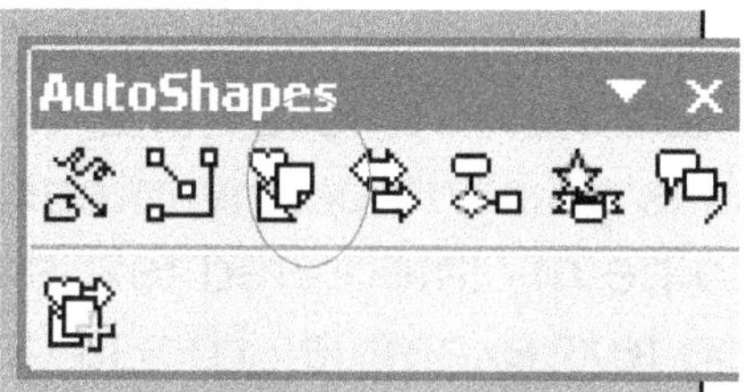

Click autoshapes

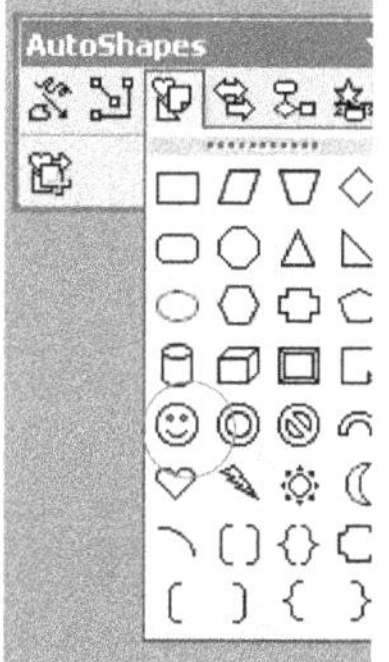

Double click on the one you want

And that's it

Integrating pictures with text

This is going to be my integrated text example. This is going to be my integrated text example. This is going to be my integrated text example. This is going to be my integrated text example. This is going to be my integrated text example. This is going to be my integrated text example. This is going to be my integrated text example. This is going to be my integrated text example. This is going to be my integrated text example.

Insert a picture like shown earlier- 

This is going to be my integrated text example. This is going to be my integrated text example. This is going to be my integrated text example. This is going to be my integrated text example. This is going to be my integrated text example. This is going to be my integrated text example. This is going to be my integrated text example. This is going to be my integrated text example. This is going to be my integrated text example.

This is my integrated text example. This is my integrated text example. This is my integrated text example. My integrated text example. This is my integrated text example. This is my integrated text example. This is my integrated text example. This is my integrated text example. This is my integrated text example.

Drag the picture into the text

You're finished

Creating Tables

1st go to tables

2nd a drop down menu will appear
Go to insert then go to table. A pop up
Will appear.

3rd adjust the number of rows and columns you want

Insert Table
Table size
Number of columns:
Number of rows: 2
AutoFit behavior
Fixed column width: Auto
AutoFit to contents
AutoFit to window
Table style: Table Grid AutoFormat...
Remember dimensions for new tables
OK Cancel

4th click ok

OK Cancel

How to shade a cell in a table.

1st Insert a table as shown on the previous page.

2nd right click on the corner of the table on a box like this:

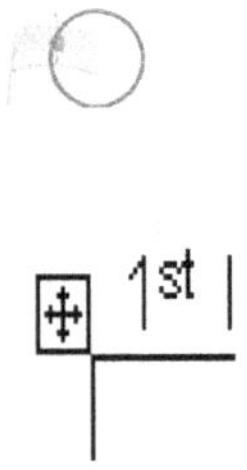

3rd a pop up will appear. Click borders and shading

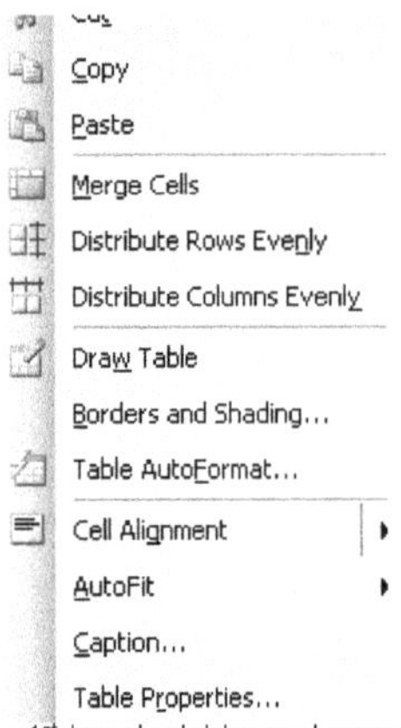

4th pick your colour and click ok.

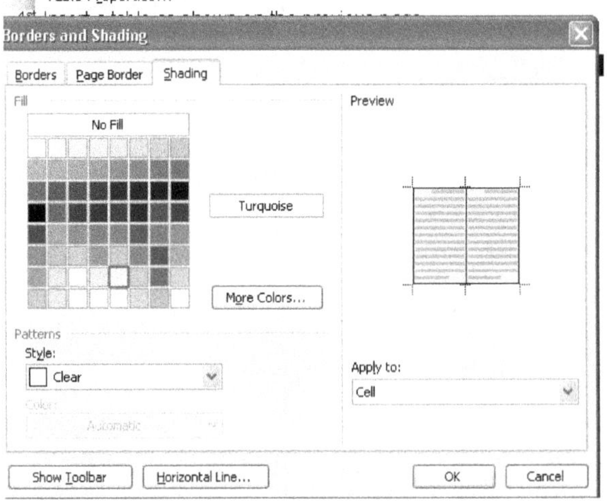

5th and you're done.

Adjusting cell alignment.

cat	cat	cat	cat	cat
dog	dog	dog	dog	dog

1st do up to step 3 but instead of clicking borders and shading click cell alignment.

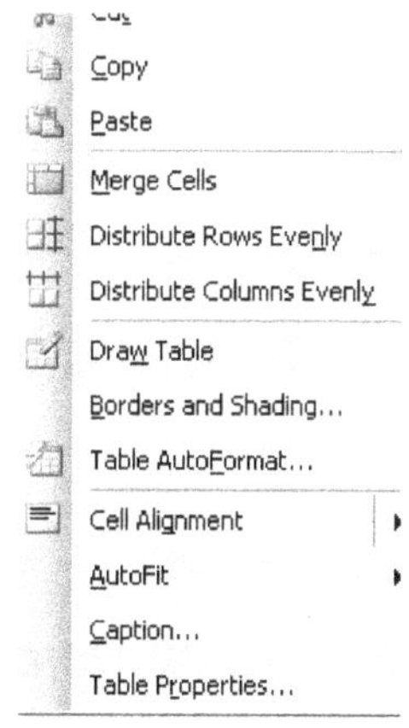

2nd select the option you want.

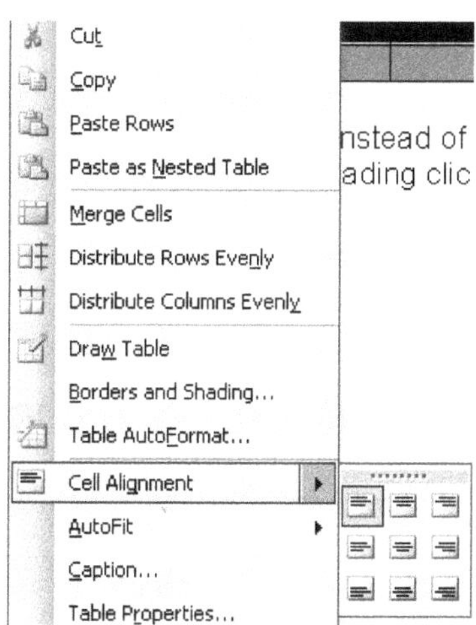

3rd and you are done

cat	cat	cat	cat	cat
dog	dog	dog	dog	dog

Adding an extra row to your table.

1st insert a table

cat	cat	cat	cat	cat
dog	dog	dog	dog	dog

2nd click table

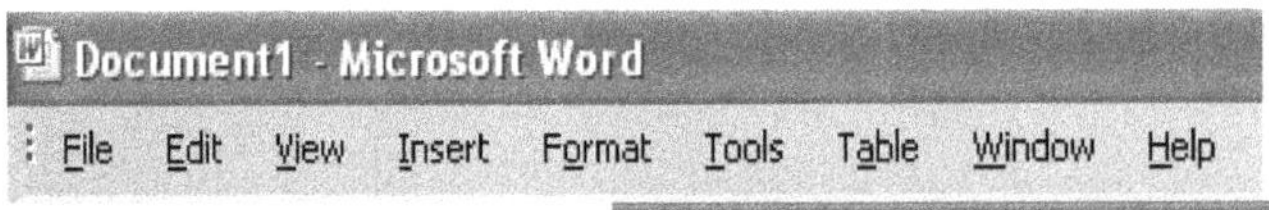

Document1 - Microsoft Word
File Edit View Insert Format Tools Table Window Help

3rd click insert on the table menu

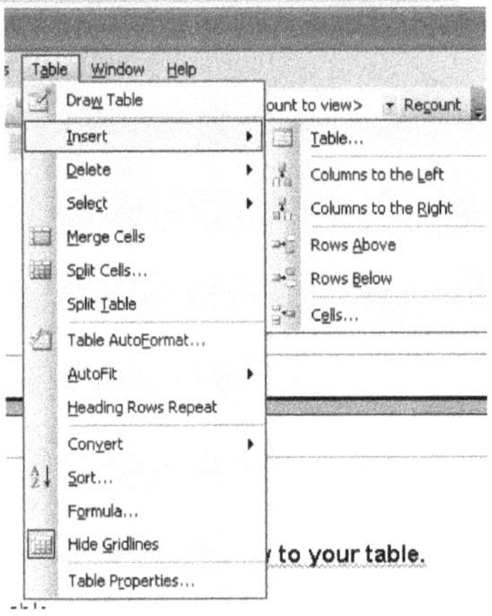

Table Window Help
Draw Table
Insert
Delete
Select
Merge Cells
Split Cells...
Split Table
Table AutoFormat...
AutoFit
Heading Rows Repeat
Convert
Sort...
Formula...
Hide Gridlines
Table Properties...
Table...
Columns to the Left
Columns to the Right
Rows Above
Rows Below
Cells...

4th click rows below/above depending on your choice.

cat	cat	cat	cat	cat
dog	dog	dog	dog	dog

5th and you are finished.

Deleing rows/columns

cat	cat	cat	cat	cat
dog	dog	dog	dog	dog

1st do up to step 2

2nd instead of clicking Insert click delete.

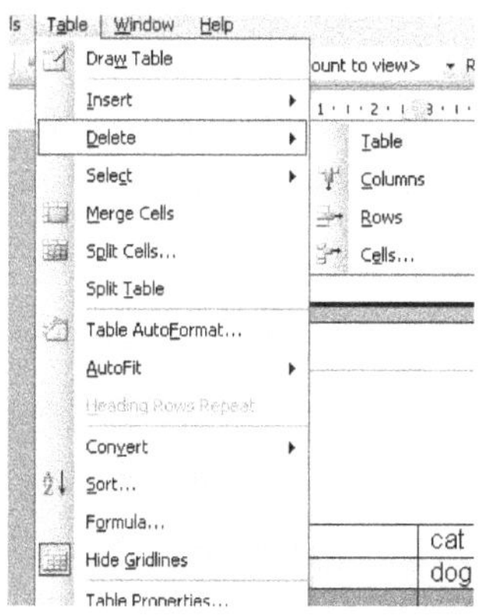

3rd select the option You want.

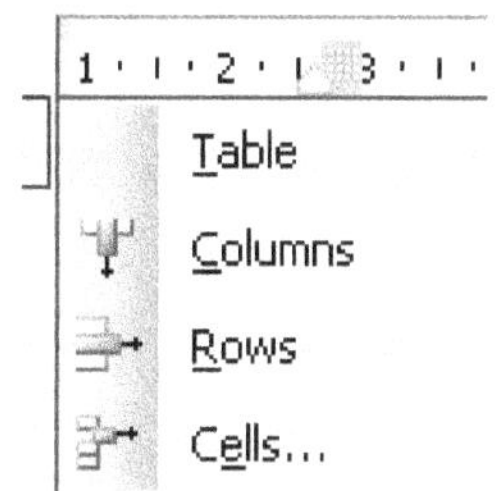

4th and you're finished

cat	cat	cat	cat	cat
dog	dog	dog	dog	dog

Use of tables to organise content.

football scores-

Brentford v Stockport 1-0
Bradford v Hereford 1-0
Bury v Rotherham 0-1

1st insert a table.

Name of winning team	vs.	Losing team	Score	-	score
Brentford	vs.	Stockport	1	-	0
Bradford	vs.	Hereford	1	-	0
Bury	vs.	Rotherham	0	-	1

2nd fill in the table

3rd you're finished look at the difference

football scores-

Brentford v Stockport 1-0
Bradford v Hereford 1-0
Bury v Rotherham 0-1

Name of winning team	vs.	Losing team	Score	-	score
Brentford	vs.	Stockport	1	-	0
Bradford	vs.	Hereford	1	-	0
Bury	vs.	Rotherham	0	-	1

Insert automatic date and time

1st go to insert.

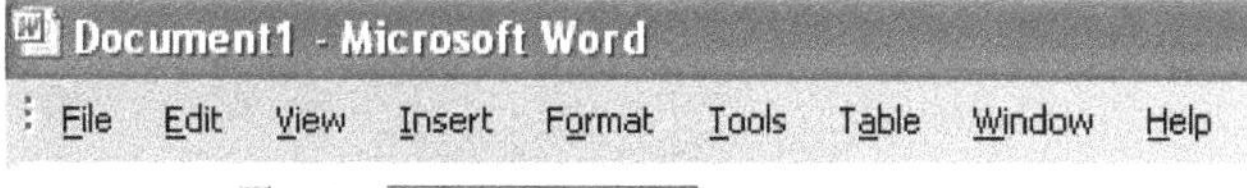

2nd go to date and time.

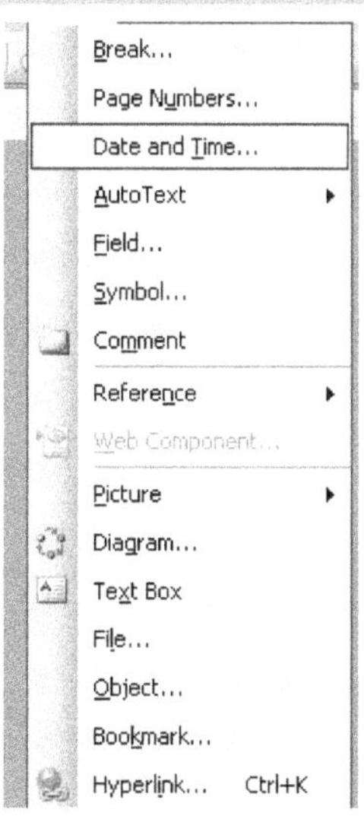

3rd select your options.

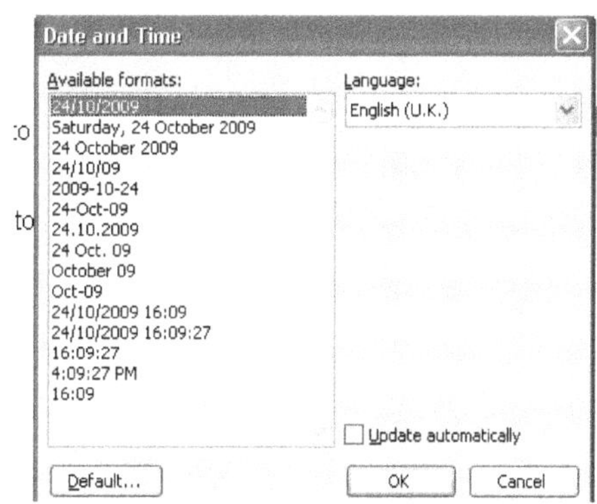

4th and that's it

24/10/2009 16:11:15

Insert page numbers

1st go to insert

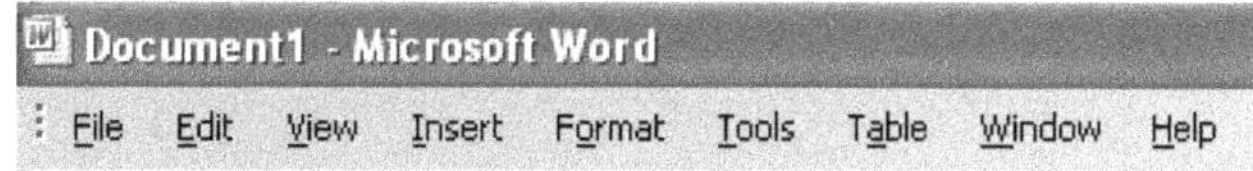

2nd go to page numbers

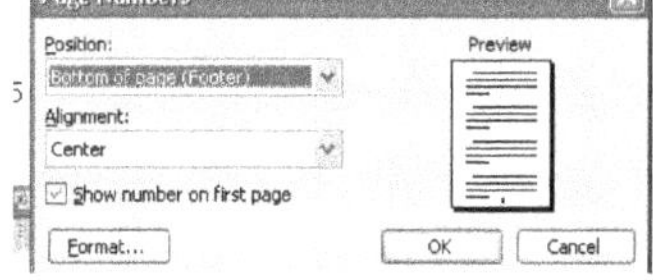

3rd select your options

4th and you're finished

Insert border

1st go to format

2nd borders and shading

3rd click the page borders tab

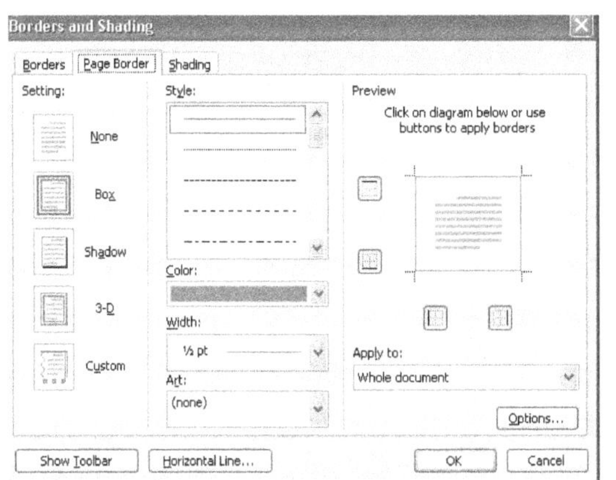

4th select your options

5th and you're finished

Changing page margins

1st go to file

2nd a menu
Will appear

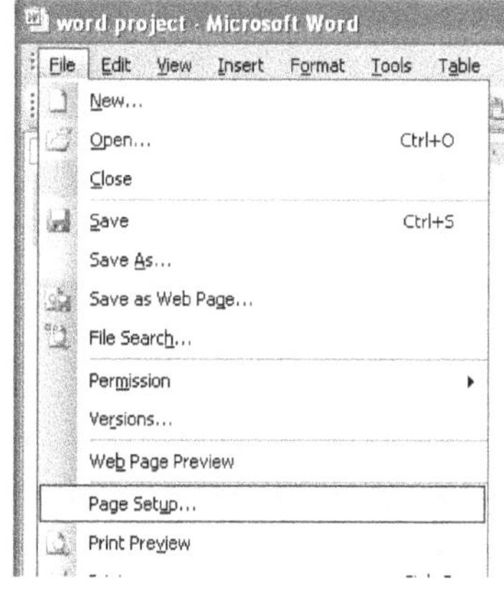

3rd click page
Setup

4th choose
Your options
see
The next 2 pages
for an example

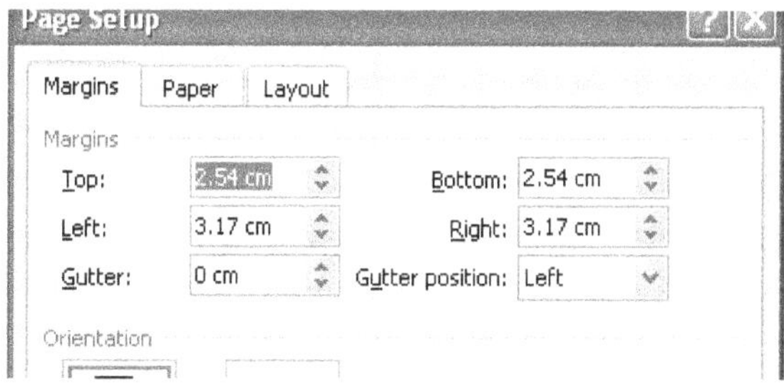

This is the text not affected by a margin
This is the text not affected by a margin
This is the text not affected by a margin
This is the text not affected by a margin
This is the text not affected by a margin
This is the text not affected by a margin

After you select your options the text should move up down left or right.

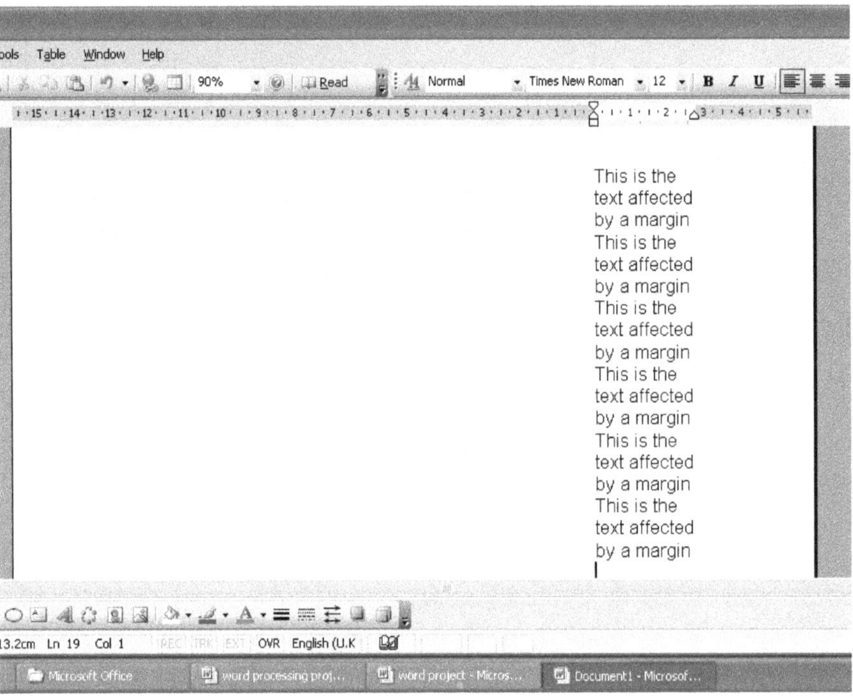

And you're done

please note that the margin will affect the whole document not just 1 page

Page orientation

1st Go to file

2nd page Setup

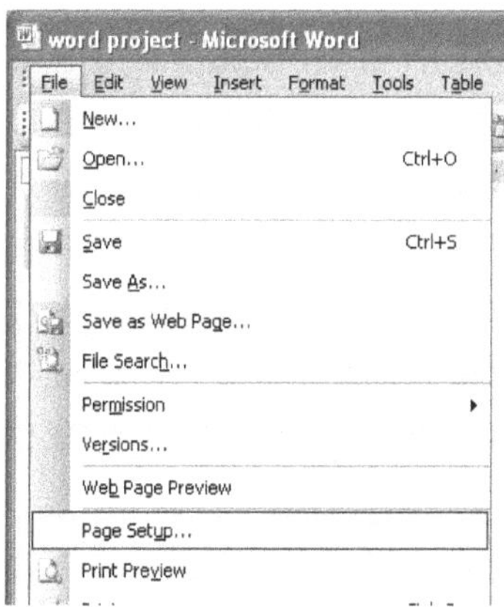

3rd click either portrait or landscape

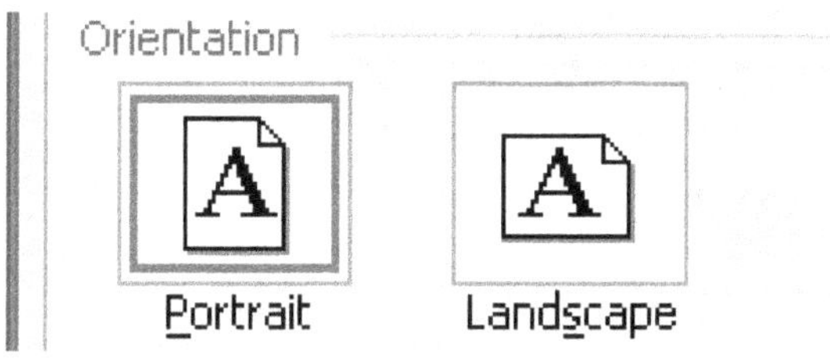

Portrait looks like this and landscape looks like this.

Do you like my book? Do you like my book? Do you like my book? Do you like my book? Do you like my book? Do you like my book?	Of course u do. Of course u do. Of course u do. Of course u do. Of course u do. Of course u do. Of course u do.

And you're finished

Text spacing

1st type your text in this case mine is:
The quick brown fox jumped over the moon
The quick brown fox jumped over the moon
The quick brown fox jumped over the moon
The quick brown fox jumped over the moon
The quick brown fox jumped over the moon
The quick brown fox jumped over the moon

2nd highlight the text by right clicking and then dragging

The quick brown fox jumped over the moon
The quick brown fox jumped over the moon
The quick brown fox jumped over the moon
The quick brown fox jumped over the moon
The quick brown fox jumped over the moon
The quick brown fox jumped over the moon

3rd right click a menu will appear

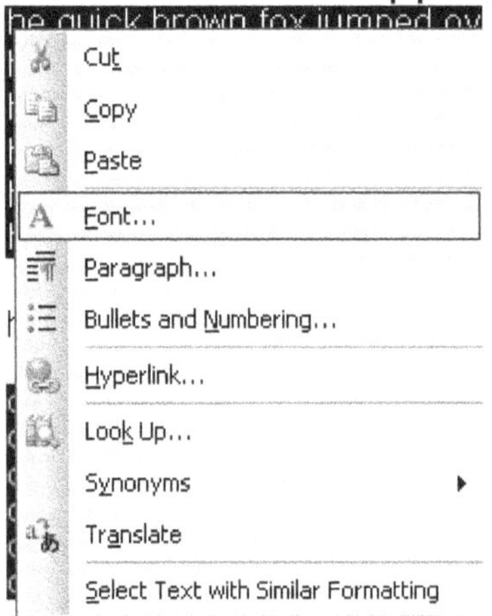

4th click font a popup will open

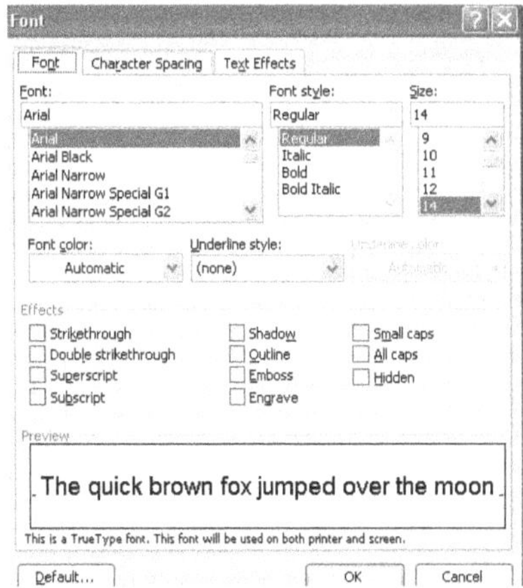

5th click the second tab character spacing

.

6th a new page will appear

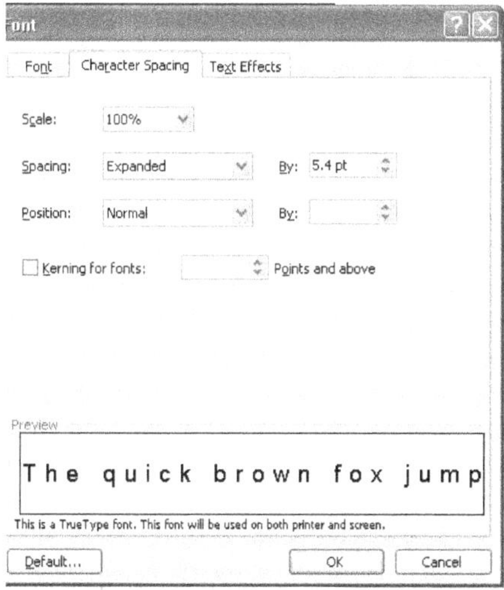

7th select your options

8th afterwards your text should look like this.

The quick brown fox jump

9th and you're finished.

Deleting text

1st Type your text:

Oops I made a mistakes

2nd find your mistake
S is mine
3rd highlight the text like earlier

stakes

4th press backspace

5th and you have finished

Oops I made a mistake

Moving text

1st write your text

How to move text

2nd highlight it

How to move text

2nd highlight it

3rd drag the text to where you want it

4th a weird dotted line appears that is where your text will be placed

How to move text

And that's it your done

Text justification

1st type your text

I want this text to be justified

2nd highlight them

I want this text to be justified

3rd click this button

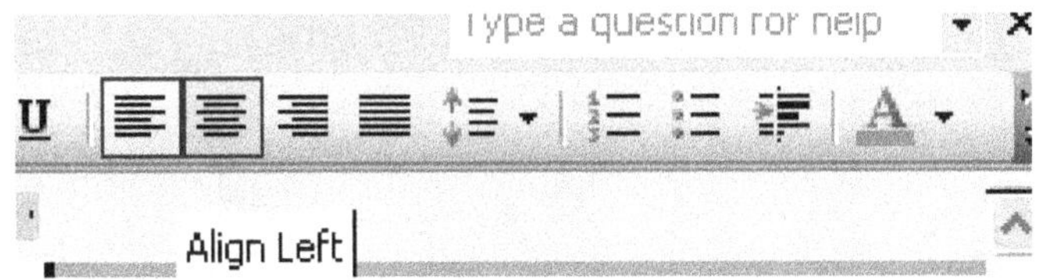

5th and you text changes like this

I want this text to be justified

And you're finished

How to insert bullets

1st go to format

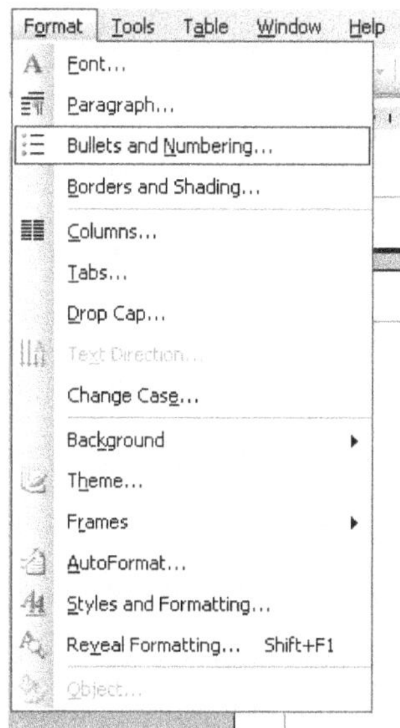

2nd bullets and numbers

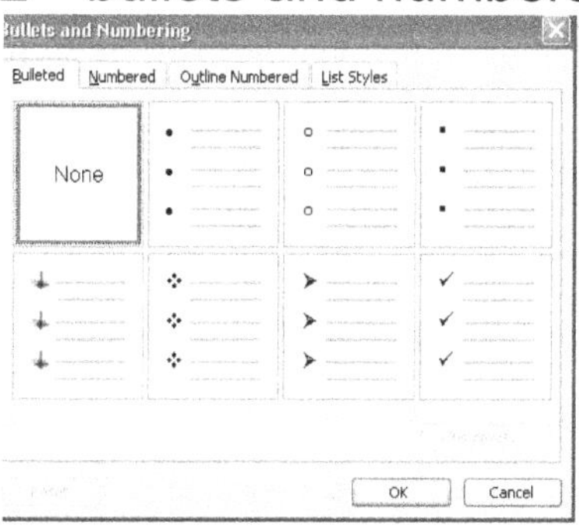

3rd select the one

4th This is the list I want to add bullets to:

Iced tea
Coca cola
Sprite
Fanta
Water

5th and click ok

- Iced tea
- Coca cola
- Sprite
- Fanta
- Water

And thats it.

Change the font/size

1st type your text:

This is my plain old boring text

2nd then go to this menu

3rd click the arrow then select your fonts

4th and your text will change

This is my plain old boring text
……..NOT

Change the size

1st highlight the text

2nd instead of clicking the fonts dropdown menu click the size one beside it.

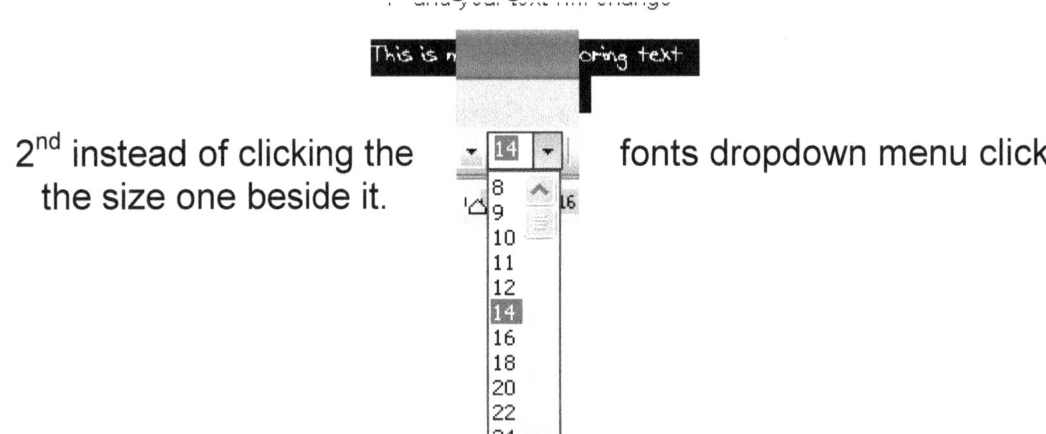

3rd Select your size

4th your font will change

This is my plain old boring text
........NOT

And youre done

A note from the author

Word should be easy to use not some over complicated piece of software this was an IT homework and I just decided to get it home published. All I want is for people to understand computers more as they are very important in life.

NOTES

NOTES

NOTES

NOTES

NOTES

NOTES

NOTES

NOTES

NOTES

NOTES

NOTES

NOTES

NOTES

NOTES

NOTES

NOTES

NOTES

NOTES

NOTES

NOTES

NOTES

NOTES

NOTES

NOTES

NOTES

NOTES

NOTES

NOTES

NOTES

NOTES

NOTES

NOTES

NOTES

NOTES

NOTES

NOTES

NOTES

NOTES

NOTES

NOTES

NOTES

NOTES

NOTES

NOTES

NOTES

NOTES

NOTES

NOTES

NOTES

NOTES

NOTES

NOTES

NOTES

NOTES

NOTES

NOTES

NOTES

NOTES

NOTES

NOTES

NOTES

NOTES

NOTES

NOTES

NOTES

NOTES

www.ingramcontent.com/pod-product-compliance
Lightning Source LLC
Chambersburg PA
CBHW081226050326
40689CB00016B/3700
* 9 7 8 1 4 4 5 2 2 5 6 7 8 *